PET OWNER'S GUIDE TO THE
GREYHOUND

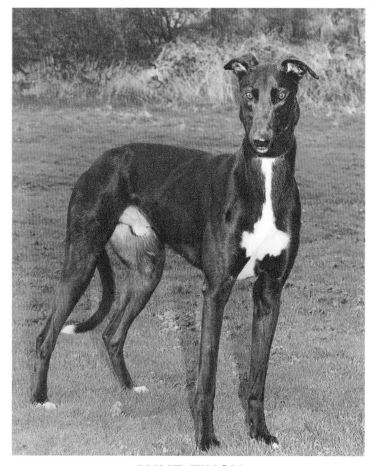

ANNE FINCH

Photography: Steve Nash

RINGPRESS

I dedicate this book to all those hard-working homefinders and generous owners who recognise the true nature of the Greyhound. The appeal of these beautiful, gentle, and undemanding dogs moves us all to defend them, and to fight for a fairer deal for Greyhounds worldwide.

ABOUT THE AUTHOR

Anne Finch, a qualified nurse of some thirty years standing, first became involved in Greyhounds when she adopted Emma, a stray dog. Like so many Greyhounds, Emma proved to be a devoted, patient and loving companion. She was a former racer, and it was by studying her history through her ear-marks, that Anne discovered the world of racing Greyhounds, and the tremendous need to find homes for retired dogs. Since that time Anne has been a tireless campaigner on behalf of former racing Greyhounds and has been responsible for finding homes for many hundreds of Greyhounds. She has taken a special interest in Greyhounds that race in Spain, and she has organised rehoming schemes for Spanish and British dogs in a number of European countries, including Germany.

ACKNOWLEDGEMENTS

My greatest thanks go to my husband, 'poor Arthur', for putting up with me and my Greyhound work, for reading the manuscript, and for doing all the cooking and the housework. Thanks must also go to Runnymede Hill Veterinary Hospital, Egham, Surrey, to Dr Roger Mugford of The Company of Animals, Chertsey, for checking over the manuscript. Thanks to Sally Ann Thompson and Colin Riley for supplying photographs.

Published by Ringpress Books,
Vincent Lane, Dorking, Surrey,
RH4 3YX, England.

First published 1997
© Interpet Publishing. All rights reserved

ISBN 1 86054 077 5
Printed in Hong Kong through Printworks Int. Ltd.

CONTENTS

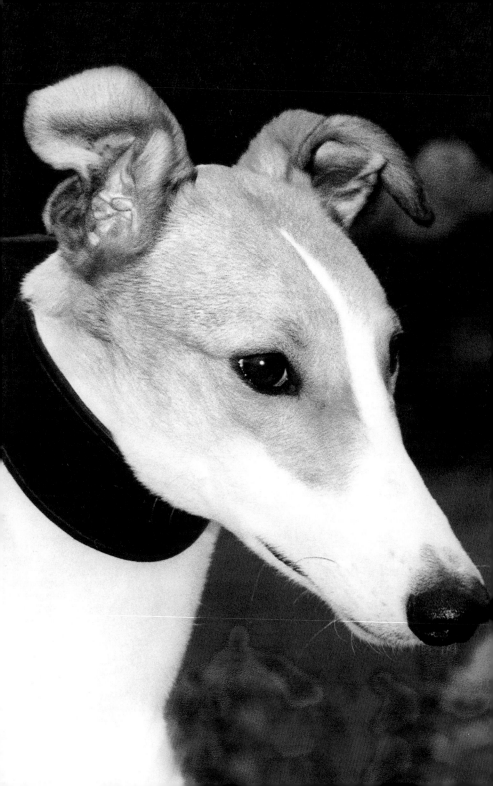

Introducing Greyhounds

W hat is a Greyhound? The breed is classified as one of the sighthounds whose ancestry dates back to many centuries BC – it is the only breed of dog mentioned in the Bible, where the Greyhound is one of four things 'comely in going' (Authorised Version, Proverbs, 30:29-31). Ovid and Arrian, writers of Roman times, documented in some detail the sport of coursing the hare with a couple of Greyhounds.

The origin of the word Greyhound has puzzled many. It may have meant 'Greek hound', or 'gre hound' meaning of high rank, or 'grach hund' meaning dog hunter, or even a corruption of 'gaze hound' meaning that the dog hunts by sight. Words can be reshaped over the centuries in order to make them seem logical, obscuring their true origins. The present Greyhound probably descends from the Canis Gallicus, or Celtic Hound, from France.

The Spanish Greyhound, the Galgo, is very similar to our own and obviously derives from its Gallic neighbours.

THE NOBLE GREYHOUND

In ancient times they were used both for hunting and for sport but by the 11th century in Britain, with the improvement in agriculture, laws were passed which forbade the ownership and the use of the Greyhound by commoners for hunting, in order to reserve them exclusively for noblemen for sport. At about this time the punishment for killing a Greyhound was death, as it was for murder. In Elizabeth I's time, rules for judging competition coursing were drawn up and they have barely changed since. Points are gained not for the kill but for the dog's performance while chasing the hare, which usually escapes. The sport developed in the 1700s, with the creation of coursing clubs up and down the country, and a number of eccentric aristocrats strove to breed the most perfect Greyhound. Lord Orford was the most celebrated, and he was reputed to have crossed the Greyhound with a number of breeds including the Italian Greyhound, the Lurcher and, most incredibly, the Bulldog! Admittedly the Bulldog then resembled more the Bull Terrier of today.

RACING BEGINS

The Greyhound was introduced to America and Australia with the early settlers in the late 1770s, and was used to hunt game. In the mid-19th century, emigrants brought Greyhounds and live hares to the New World specifically for coursing. The 19th century brought with it better transport facilities and more leisure time and the sport attracted more owners and enthusiastic breeders. However, the status of the Greyhound began to decline in 1906 in America, with the advent of oval track racing with an artificial lure. This was created to attract as many spectators as possible, with the added incentive of betting and bookmakers. Australia and Britain followed this trend a few years later, with tracks springing up throughout these countries. In London, the National Greyhound Racing Club was formed in 1928 to exert

The Greyhound races with boundless enthusiasm.

uniformity and discipline, protecting the integrity of the sport with its emphasis on drug testing, identity-checking and controlled kennelling. In Britain, there are now 33 tracks operating under NGRC rules and 40 tracks which are independent. The Bord na gCon is the ruling body in Ireland. In America the tracks are privately owned but under the control of the State Racing Commissions.

The Irish Coursing Club in Clonmel, Co. Tipperary, was founded in 1916 and houses the Irish Stud Book. The Club controls the registration of litters and the namings of the dogs. The English Stud Book at Newmarket registers the Greyhounds bred in Britain. Both Irish and English dogs are tattooed in their ears at 10 to 12 weeks with the year of birth, litter mark and place of registration. The National Greyhound Association in Abilene, Kansas, USA, and the Australian and New Zealand Greyhound Association in Melbourne, Australia, hold the Stud Books for those countries.

With the growth of Greyhound tracks, thousands more Greyhounds had to be bred in all four countries and between 1925 and 1935 the number of litters almost trebled. In the 1970s and 80s the annual number of namings in the Irish Stud Book reached 20,000 and in the English Stud book 10,000. These numbers have decreased of late, due to the recession. The Greyhound industry is in some difficulties financially, both in America and Britain. Tracks are closing as betting returns decrease. The National Lottery in Britain, and casinos in the USA, have contributed to the drop in betting money. There is said to be a shortage of dogs, due to the drop in breeding and the increased numbers of races because of the necessity to bring in more betting money to sustain the tracks. The tracks in Britain are also under obligation to invest huge sums of money in safety measures following the disaster at the Hillsborough football ground in 1989.

The thousands bred for racing are a headache for lovers of the breed who are involved in home-finding. Dogs are usually retired from racing at four years old, or even earlier, and enough homes cannot be found to accommodate all those deserving a comfortable retirement.

The coursing Greyhound is usually taller and bigger-boned.

CHARACTERISTICS

The modern breed of Greyhound is divided into three main types, the most common being the racing Greyhound, English and Irish. Their breeding has evolved since the 1920s to suit oval track racing of 400 meters or so, with four tight bends. A rapid sprinter with early pace was necessary. Irish coursing dogs were more suitable for such adaptation than their English equivalents, because coursing in Ireland was held in an enclosed space, called park coursing, where rapid acceleration was an advantage. This type of coursing was forbidden in England. Track – racing Greyhounds need to reach 37 to 43 mph within a couple of seconds. Shiploads of Irish Greyhounds were transported from Ireland to England in the 1920s for the new tracks. Selective breeding, with preferred stud dogs, evolved them into the racing dog of today. They are shorter and lighter than coursing dogs. The average height at the shoulder for a bitch is 70 cm and 74 cm for a dog. The weight varies between 23 kg and 33 kg. Greyhounds are always smooth-coated and come in black, white, brindle, fawn and blue, or white broken with any of these colours.

A typical coursing dog is taller and bigger-boned, with a deeper, broader chest and heavier legs which are more suited to longer runs and uneven terrain. It has more endurance than the track dog, as it must run at least twice in one day. The show Greyhound is nearer to the coursing Greyhound in appearance. It is bred for elegance, is flat-sided and more angular, with a deep, narrow chest, longer nose and slim head. It does not have the stamina of coursing or racing Greyhounds, nor their ability to twist and turn when running. Its colours are not so varied, being commonly white and brindle.

Greyhounds lack the usual doggy odour associated with many other breeds. Moulting is not a problem except, slightly, in some white dogs or when a dog has come from a cold kennel and therefore grown a thick coat. On coming into a warm house the dog will then moult that coat – once and for all. Some humans who are normally allergic to dogs can, in fact, live happily with a Greyhound.

The temperaments of all three types are similar – affectionate, non-aggressive and comfort-loving. However, the racing Greyhound, which has been institutionalised in a racing kennel, is mild-mannered and easy-to-handle compared to the show Greyhound which possesses the exuberance and playfulness of any other breed.

The show Greyhound is bred for elegance.

THE RACING LIFE

One thing is almost certain – if you are thinking of adopting an ex-racing Greyhound then he or she will certainly not be a puppy. Puppies are all potential racers and worth a lot of money. It is only the racing failures and the retired dogs which need homes. It is therefore useful to have some knowledge of the life of a racing Greyhound in order to understand his, or her, habits.

EARLY DAYS

Let us start at the very beginning. The partners in a mating are always considered very carefully by the breeder. One of them will probably be a celebrity, either an ex-Champion (a stud dog) or a well-known brood bitch. Often much travelling and effort is involved. Hence, you will never find a Greyhound with inherited physical or mental problems, as can happen with other breeds. A sound temperament is a hallmark of the breed. I feel much of this is due to the careful breeding, which has to be registered and made public on a race-card. Close inter-breeding is impossible.

The bitch will be whelped, and the pups reared, in kennels. At 10 to 12 weeks the pups will be tattooed in both ears if Irish, and in the right ear if English. The pups remain with their mother until 12 weeks by which time they will be fully weaned. Collars are put on them at about five months, when they must learn to walk on the lead. At 12 months they start gentle schooling. They learn to chase after a 'drag hare' for a short distance and are introduced to the starting traps. At 14 months they are kennelled with an older dog to calm them down, and at 15 months they will be trialled at the

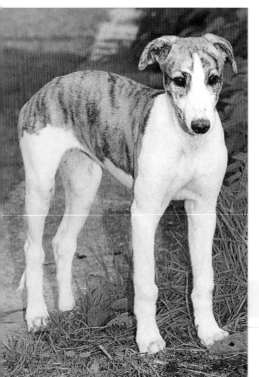

Greyhound puppies stay with their mother for the first 12 weeks.

tracks. These saplings are usually reared with lots of freedom to run and chase about, in order to develop their muscles and good turning ability.

THE RACING ROUTINE

Once their racing life begins, their exercise is disciplined to conserve energy for race days. Walking is preferred to keep them fit. The food in a racing kennel is high in protein content and of excellent quality. In the UK, Greyhounds are kennelled in pairs, usually a dog and a bitch together. They sleep on a bench with a thick bedding of straw or shredded paper. They use the concrete floor for toilet purposes and rarely soil their beds. In America, Greyhounds are usually kept separately, in two-tier cages, also with thick bedding.

In most kennels, the dogs will have about six outings each day into the paddock. During the day they may be massaged and groomed and will have their teeth and ears cleaned and their feet checked. On a race day, the trainer takes the racing dogs to the track with him. They travel either in purpose-built cages in special vans or they can be loose in private cars. They are muzzled to prevent

any interference with each other. It is a bye-law that racing dogs should be muzzled when they leave the kennels.

RACE TRACK PROCEDURE

On arrival at the track, random urine samples are taken to test for drugs. The dogs are weighed, their ear-marks are checked and they are kennelled, under observation, for one-and-a-half to two hours before the first race in order to protect them from any interference by drugs. Just before racing their ear-marks are checked again. This frequent examination of the ears may explain why some retired dogs hate their ears being touched – previous rough handling may have sensitised them.

Six dogs usually run in a race in the UK; in America there are usually eight. When the race is due, the dogs are paraded on the track by being walked on the lead in front of the spectators. They are then put in the traps without their collars. The mechanical hare is usually a soft toy. The hare starts at some distance behind the traps and, as the whirring noise approaches, this causes uncontrollable excitement and the Greyhounds burst out of the traps with an obvious thrill for the chase. The average race lasts only 30 seconds and the dogs run at speeds up to 40 mph. It is obvious, when you see the dogs coming off the track with sand on their faces and panting profusely, that they have run with all their might. They only race once or twice a week because of the huge exertion demanded of them.

RACING IN AMERICA

American Greyhounds and their racing life are comparable to the UK but with one or two differences. American Greyhounds, despite originally coming from English/Irish stock, are known to be more docile, and more laid-back, than those in the UK. The essential difference probably arises because the dogs in America are bred for stamina, the shortest race being 550 yards, whereas English and Irish dogs are bred for speed and sprint capability as races are commonly 440 metres and can be as short as 230 metres. Paddock life is also different. In America, and also in Spain, the Greyhounds are let out into the paddock in scores, all males or all females together. They are muzzled and supervised by a trainer who watches carefully and who cracks a whip on the ground in case of trouble. Drug testing is not carried out before the race, but two out of the eight dogs are randomly tested after the race.

They're off! Six Greyhounds sprint from the traps.

There are no 'flapping' tracks in the United States, operating independently of racing rules, as there are in the UK.

RACING INJURIES

Injuries are common to feet and legs. The dogs go round the track counter-clockwise and, as they negotiate the bends, their bodies lean inwards towards the centre of the track while their feet try to maintain equilibrium by gripping the ground. These injuries may be stresses and tears to ligaments and tendons and even fractures of the toes, wrists and hocks. Neck injuries can be incurred at the end of the race when the hare stops and the handlers have to catch the dogs. These injuries are usually not severe enough to affect a dog which is adopted as a pet, as he will not be so physically stressed ever again, but you might notice him limping slightly after exercise.

The person who will know your dog's racing form is his trainer and, if known, you can gain valuable information about your dog's injuries from him. A good trainer will gladly look over your dog for you and his experience with Greyhounds can be a welcome contribution towards a

In a race, Greyhounds reach speeds of up to 40mph.

correct diagnosis. When an injury causes a dog to slow up, even by as little as one second, then he may be retired. This usually happens at any age between two and five years. The life-span of a Greyhound can be 12 to 15 years, so you can be assured of many years of healthy companionship with a retired racing Greyhound.

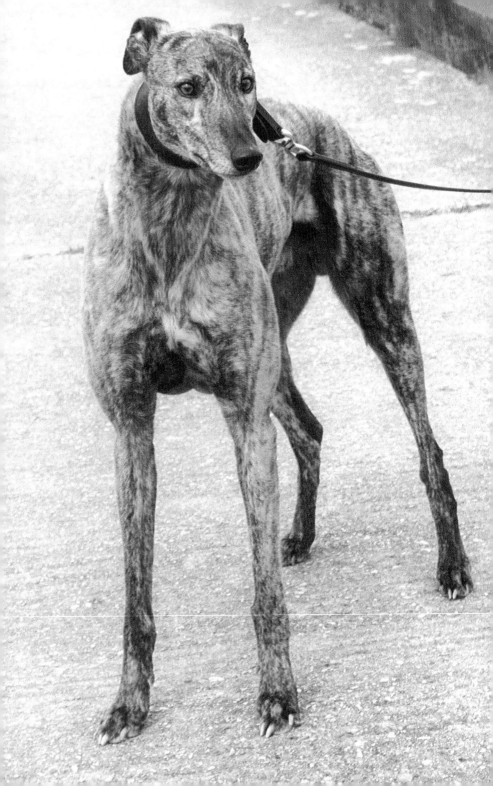

Adopting a Greyhound

There are various sources from which you can find a retired Greyhound. Most dog refuges will be likely to have Greyhounds. They may have been picked up by the police as strays or gifted to the refuge by the racing owner or trainer, or even by a previous pet owner, who no longer wants the dog. Many refuges charge for adopting one of their dogs, but this is usually to cover the costs they have incurred through spaying or castrating, worming and vaccinating and, often, micro-chipping the dog. Considering how much all this would cost you at a veterinary surgery, it is a bargain. Refuges rely entirely on charitable donations.

In the UK, the Retired Greyhound Trust is a national organisation with voluntary helpers attached to most registered tracks. Either their headquarters, or a track racing manager, would direct you to your local representatives, or you may find their advertisement in your local paper. These dogs are free, but may not be vaccinated or neutered. If there are only Independent tracks in your area, their racing office would be able to direct you to the place where you can adopt one of their retired dogs. Some trainers find homes for their dogs themselves. They are frequently left with retired racers on their hands. Their homing procedures are more informal, but they know their dogs well and they will usually take a dog back if the homing does not work out satisfactorily.

There are other voluntary groups of dedicated Greyhound lovers who help by finding homes and promoting Greyhounds as pets. They advertise locally in the UK, and in the USA and Canada there is a large directory of Greyhound Adoption organisations; some advertise on the Internet. Smaller groups are springing up in Germany, Belgium and Switzerland where professional Greyhound racing does not exist. These kind people have offered to adopt retired Greyhounds from the UK and from Spain, where Irish Greyhounds are exported for racing.

HOME VISITING

If you are offering a home you will – or you should be – asked to complete a questionnaire, and a home visit will probably be made by a Greyhound owner who will talk to you about the dog's special needs. It is best if the whole family is present when the home visitor comes; all members of the family should have discussed together the idea of adopting a Greyhound and all, ideally, should be equally keen. However, we all know of situations where one partner has been uncertain at the outset but then becomes thoroughly enchanted and dedicated once the dog has found its way into his or her heart. The home visitor will discuss the suitability of your premises and your work hours.

FAMILY CONSIDERATIONS

If you have young children, or you are planning to start a family, think carefully before undertaking to adopt a dog. It is upsetting for the children, and for the dog – especially one as sensitive as a Greyhound – if it has to be rejected from its new home when the added commitment proves too much. Think beforehand how you will cope with a push-chair, pouring rain, and the dog who needs exercise. The rejected dog may have been driven to soil in the house or snap at unsupervised, over-boisterous children, and then, unfairly, retains that label when it re-admitted to kennels, making rehoming very difficult.

It is essential to bear in mind that your attention will be required at all times when the dog and the children are together. This is to protect the dog from too much rough attention, and to tell the children when it is time to leave the dog alone so that it can go to sleep. A play-pen is useful for toddlers and, equally, a crate for your Greyhound will provide a safe haven, and allow you to to get on with your work. On the positive side, children and dogs make wonderful companions; they learn about caring and dependence; for a withdrawn or shy child, or an only child, the dog may be its dearest companion.

Take a look at your family. If

Greyhounds make wonderful family pets.

you are noisy, dynamic and easy-going, then consider a bolder dog. If you are quieter and more orderly, then consider a more sensitive dog. A very boisterous or very nervous dog would not be suitable for a young family. If the children go to school, the dog can have a rest from the rough and tumble, and you can devote time to him during those hours. Exercise him so he is relaxed and comfortable when the children

return from school and the rumpus begins. Be sensitive to when the dog has had enough of the children. It is natural, for instance, for a bitch to snap at her pups when she has had enough of them. She will not bite, but it is a warning to you to separate the children and the harassed dog.

Much is spoken of the dangers of the toxocara worm and blindness in children. It is extremely rare and, above all,

With careful supervision, children and Greyhounds can become great friends.

easily preventable with six-monthly worming. Toxocara eggs are found everywhere in the ground, not just in a dog, so regular handwashing at all times is a must for children.

You will need to involve your children in all aspects of training your dog. They must remember to keep the garden gate closed; they should be able to teach your dog to stay, especially on opening a car door; they should use the correct toilet command, stay with him in the garden while he does so and then reward him; they should be taught to groom their pet and should be involved in their pet's feeding and veterinary care. This is a very good way of educating the children in the workings of a mammal and in general health matters.

INTRODUCING A BABY

Introducing a new baby needs thought and preparation. When the new baby arrives, your dog will be relegated in favour of the newcomer, so prepare the dog during the preceding months – otherwise the dog is bound to feel jealous if he is suddenly ignored. Accustom your Greyhound to spending time on his own when you are in the house, and adjust sleeping arrangements, if necessary, in advance. It is a good idea to let your Greyhound hear the sound of a baby crying – either by visiting friends with babies, or taking him to sit outside a baby clinic. If the Greyhound is not prepared in advance, the sound of a baby crying could trigger the hunting instinct. When you return from hospital with your baby, make a big fuss of your dog, and then allow him to sniff the baby. In this way, the newcomer will quickly be accepted as one of the family. Never leave your baby and dog together unsupervised.

A GREYHOUND'S NEEDS

The basic needs are the same when adopting any dog as a pet. The height of fencing and security, however, are especially important for Greyhounds, as they can jump six feet when motivated, though they are usually too lazy! If the lower four feet of the fence is opaque then the dog may not necessarily see the cat or rabbit next door and two feet of open trellis fastened on to the top of your fence may be more acceptable to you if you do not like to feel too enclosed. The home visitor will be interested in how much of the day the dog will be alone: more than five hours is really too long. He or she will point out the conditions of the contract that you will sign on adopting the dog, which will safeguard the dog's welfare and future. The dog should always wear an identity disc; the dog should be regularly wormed and vaccinated throughout its

You must have enough time to spend with your adopted Greyhound.

21

life; the dog should not be raced, bred from or used for profit, and, should this adoption not be successful, the dog should be returned to the homing organisation.

Some organisations arrange annual reunions which give everyone the opportunity to show off their dogs, talk Greyhounds and share experiences. Equipment and other goods can be sold to help raise money for the group. For the group leaders, these are important events for reassuring them of the happiness and well-being of their dogs.

DIRECT REHOMING

If your dog is being rehomed and coming from his previous home direct to you, then try to bring some of his own things with him, such as his feeding bowl, bed cover, collar, lead and any toys he may have. Do not forget his vaccination certificate. He will be confused, so do not be too much of a disciplinarian; stay with him the first night and be patient if he takes a while to settle. These dogs are very sensitive and every time they move homes they have a minor nervous breakdown! Take a detailed history from the previous owners of the routine he has been used to, and their house rules. Find out to whom he related best and whether there were children, or other pets, in the household. You will then have a deeper understanding of the new challenges facing him in your home.

ADOPTING AN UNKNOWN

In some situations you may know absolutely nothing about your new dog. If he is tattooed then you can find out from the correct Stud Book his racing name and age. If, in addition, he is registered with the NGRC, you can trace the track where he raced and, thus, his trainer. You may be able to find

Male Greyhounds can be harder to rehome.

out his pet name too, or guess it from his racing name. The trainer or track manager might also be able to give you information about vaccinations, seasons, temperament and whether the dog was retired because he would not chase. This sort of information is useful, as non-chasers have a better chance of finding a home quickly as they usually live easily with cats. Chasers need to be re-educated.

CHOOSING THE RIGHT DOG

You will, no doubt, have decided whether you want a dog or a bitch. If you already have an entire male dog at home then you should think carefully. Bringing in another uncastrated male dog can lead to fighting, though I do know of several male dogs who live together without incident. If you bring in a female then she should be spayed – keeping male and female apart for three weeks during her season can be a nightmare. There are other health advantages to spaying and castration which we will discuss later. It must be said, however, that any surgical operation carries with it some risks. They are rare but are tragic when they occur.

In the UK we find it more difficult to home a male dog, mainly because of his larger size, so we are delighted when someone will consider a male. In America this preference does not occur, maybe because their houses are larger. People also think that a bitch would be more affectionate

than a dog but, in fact, a Greyhound male is not especially 'macho' and can be as loving and gentle as any female. Male Greyhounds can actually be quite entertaining as, dare I say it, they have a sense of humour!

You need to decide whether a bouncy or a more placid dog is for you, or whether you would be dedicated enough to adopt a very nervous dog. Some people like a dog with plenty of spirit, while others prefer the peace-loving type. An elderly person could cope well with a typically well-mannered quiet Greyhound. Noisy, energetic children would upset such a dog. While on the subject of a suitable dog for small children, avoid a Greyhound with one of those amazing tails which whips round through three

hundred and sixty degrees, flaying everything in its path! They are not common, but we once had to rehome a dog because the child's face was at the level of the tail which, in addition, had a sclerosed injury at the tip, like a marble.

It is a sad fact that some elderly dogs of ten years or more find themselves homeless, either when a racing kennel must close and the 'resters' cannot be accommodated any longer, or when someone's domestic circumstances change. These older dogs are adorable and you can take enormous pleasure in nursing them in their old age and being able to contribute towards a comfortable end to their lives.

ESSENTIAL EQUIPMENT
The first thing you will want to do on receiving your Greyhound is to

bath him – so you will need the equipment recommended in the section on Fleas (Chapter Three). Even if he has not got fleas, he may smell of kennels. Pet shops are not the best places in which to find equipment for Greyhounds. A specialised Greyhound supplier is the ideal source. Your local Greyhound rescue group will know of one, or ask your local track or trainer.

BED AND BEDDING

There is an expense at the outset. A suitable bed must be provided to which the dog can retreat without interference. I have tried every kind of bed available and now favour a round or oval foam bed with two-inch thick walls and a removable, washable fur-fabric cover. A bed can be improvised with a double duvet folded over or with a couple of settee cushions,

covered with washable blankets. These can be bought at second-hand markets for next to nothing. The most important requirement is that the bed is soft, or your dog will suffer from sores on his bony joints. Americans are more used to the idea of an indoor kennel or crate, and they are becoming increasingly popular in the UK. The kennel should never be used as a punishment cell, nor should the children be allowed in it. It is the dog's treasured place of rest providing security, comfort and a retreat from the family. A quiet draught-free corner of the room, or a place under the stairs away from the general traffic, are favoured places for a bed or den.

FEEDING BOWL

You will need a large feeding bowl, at least nine inches across. The male dogs require something akin to a small washing-up bowl for the correct daily quantity of food. You will also need a separate water bowl.

COLLAR

You will need to buy a Greyhound collar. We use leather, fish-shaped collars, wide in the middle. When you first meet your dog you should fasten it really quite cosily just behind the ears – the narrowest part of the neck. If your dog is small you may even have to make some new holes to tighten it sufficiently. Greyhounds are adept at wriggling backwards out of their collars, either in panic at having to cope with something unfamiliar such as entering a house for the first time, or at the attractive sight of a small

You will need a leather collar, specially designed for a Greyhound.

animal running away like a lure!

IDENTITY DISC

An identity disc with your telephone number is essential right from the moment you first meet your dog. Dogs in transit are at their most vulnerable. If you want to take off the leather collar in your house, then the dog must wear a lighter nylon collar with the disc attached. In the early days, the dog may feel insecure in your house and seize any opportunity to dash out of the front door when you open it momentarily to put out the rubbish or the milk bottles. For some dedicated escapologists it can be a good idea to fit a child's safety gate across the door (these, too, can be obtained very cheaply second-hand.)

Unfortunately, dogs do get stolen, so never leave your dog tied up outside a shop, and never leave him in a unlocked car. Consider having your Greyhound micro-chipped, and then if he is recovered, you will be reunited with the minimum of delay.

LEASH

I favour a one-inch wide cotton twill leash of about 44 inches, with a strong trigger fastener, the advantage being that you can wind it round your hand and be prepared for any lurch forward which your dog may suddenly make. Greyhounds are so well-mannered on the lead that there is no tension whatever on it, so you can be cajoled into complacency and then caught out if your hound sees something move on the horizon and bursts forward at 30 mph to investigate! The limited length gives you good control and prevents prey-pouncing into hedges. As you become more confident you could invest in an extending lead (the longest length) for use in parks and open spaces.

MUZZLE

A Greyhound muzzle is also useful to keep handy for a visit to the vet, where other clients may be carrying a cat in their arms or allowing their tortoise to run over the waiting-room floor. It is also useful as a precautionary measure when introducing your dog to your parrot, your cat, or your mother-in-law's Yorkie, or when letting your dog off the lead for the first time in a public place. These cautionary measures need not frighten you. Not all Greyhounds are so 'keen' and most settle down rapidly to domestic life. Remember, you are undoing all their previous training and, until your dog knows what is expected of him you must make sure there are no accidents on the way. He will want to please you and you will find him a devoted, malleable, quiet pet who shows immense gratitude to you for allowing him to share your life, so help him adjust with kindness and understanding.

COAT

Further items to add to the wardrobe are a fleece-lined waterproof walking-out coat and, possibly, a woollen coat or sweater for night time if you turn your heating off in the winter overnight. Feeling the insides of his earflaps will tell you if he is cold or not.

GROOMING EQUIPMENT

You will need a grooming brush for a short-haired dog. The rubber glove variety with raised pimples is suitable, as it massages at the same time.

INSURANCE

Finally, I cannot stress enough the importance of pet insurance. In the UK, it is reasonably priced, but in much of Europe the very idea is out of the question financially. However, if you take out an insurance policy, you will not regret it. Greyhounds are mainly free from genetic disease but they have a very thin skin and are accident-prone. One local Greyhound I know, called Frank, fell down his own hole in his own garden which he was excavating to Australia and broke his hock! He cost his devoted owner a small fortune in vet bills. She has taken out insurance now, but how she wishes she had invested in it before.

THE FIRST FEW DAYS

From puppyhood your Greyhound has always lived with other Greyhounds in a racing kennel and going into your home, away from them, is like landing on the moon. Many domestic appliances and structures may be frightening to him; for example the vacuum cleaner, electric mixer, television and stairs. Your sofa and bed are just like his bench in the kennel and his first instinct will be to jump up on to it. The floor was always his toilet – more about that later. Stairs are terrifying. The dog can be easily taught, however, by wrapping a towel under his stomach, holding both ends like a shopping bag, and supporting him while you lead him, firmly, upstairs. (Ideal for the purpose is a Greyhound weighing-harness which we acquired originally in order to carry our old paralysed Labrador in her last days.) Take him downstairs next. Repeat the procedure up and down a few times until he gains confidence. Getting another dog to demonstrate also works miracles.

Domestic hazards are plate-glass windows and patio doors. Introduce these to your Greyhound before he breaks through them one day after a squirrel at the end of the garden. Put an obstacle such as a chair or settee in front of them to start with, to give the dog time to get used to the idea of glass.

When your Greyhound first comes into your house he may pant and be very restless. He may cry all of the first night! Until he has experienced your 24-hour regime he will be very insecure and troubled. You will get a better night's sleep yourself if you have him in your bedroom or if you sleep downstairs with him. A child's safety-gate across your bedroom door, with him on his bed on the landing, may suit you best if you do not want him in your bedroom. He may whine when you are out of sight. For this reason, receive your dog, if possible, when you can devote a few days solely to him, to ease him into his new life. After two or three nights he will settle.

Caring For Your Greyhound

In racing kennels the dogs are fed fresh food, usually a stew of meat and vegetables cooked in a huge boiler. This is then mixed with dampened brown bread or biscuit. Any dog would welcome the continuation of this diet but, unless you have lots of time, or you eat this sort of thing yourself and would share it, it is not generally practical for the average busy household. Your friendly baker may sell you out-of-date brown bread and this would not go amiss.

There are many different types of pet food available and none is absolutely right or wrong for a Greyhound. Some very rich tinned meat causes diarrhoea but other foods – complete or dried food soaked in warm water or broth, tinned or frozen meat with mixer-biscuit – are all acceptable. It is a matter of finding one which suits your pocket, your lifestyle and your pets. I would advise you, however, not to feed a high-protein food which is designed for the racing dog. He may become over-excitable, frustrated and destructive. One of my Greyhounds in quarantine was fed a high-protein complete food and she regularly destroyed her bed and kennel coat but miraculously reformed in 48 hours with a lower-protein food.

Elderly dogs thrive better and remain more alert on higher-quality protein food like cooked chicken, fish, mutton and pasta. Old Greyhounds get scrawny with age whereas other breeds tend to get fatter. On the subject of older dogs – a raised feeding bowl will be welcomed by your dog so he does not have to stoop so low to reach his food. Simply place it on a 12 inch stool or the dishwasher or oven lid.

Introducing a new food can cause diarrhoea in the first instance until your dog's digestion gets used to it, so do not change his food again at the first sign of bowel looseness. The table on the side of the pack is a good guide to

Greyhounds should be fed smaller amounts, 2-3 times a day.

fed smaller amounts two to three times a day – we feed ours at our mealtimes. Eating is usually followed by sleeping so, if you work during the day, then arranging for him to have a meal at lunchtime will settle him for the afternoon.

It goes without saying that fresh water should be available at all times. Throughout your dog's life, watch for any significant change in his drinking habits; it can reflect your pet's general health and be a useful diagnostic aid if he becomes off-colour and your vet is looking for clues to a health problem. If flatulence is a problem, ignore this in the first few days of adoption; it is caused by nerves and will stop. However, if it occurs after that, a tablespoonful a day of natural yoghurt mixed with the food can solve the problem.

Allergic responses to food or food additives can be the cause of behavioural anomalies, anxiety, diarrhoea, and skin problems. Try controlling your Greyhound's intake by feeding only two ingredients at a time – for example, home-prepared chicken and rice, lamb and rice, or cottage cheese and potatoes. This can result in a surprisingly rapid change for the better. The

the amount you need to feed, bearing in mind the weight of your dog, which is 24 to 34 kg. If possible, find out the racing weight of your dog and keep him 2 kg heavier. You should not be able to see the pin bones on his back and should just be able to discern the outline of his three lower ribs. Greyhounds are best diagnosis is in your hands. As soon as the rogue ingredient is introduced and the old symptoms return, you have the answer to your problem.

One word of warning; Greyhounds are terrible thieves! Goodness knows why. They are not greedy and only eat what they need of their given food but stealing is a sport, so beware. They will take the bacon from the frying pan, meringues from the oven, butter from the work surface – and you may even lose your defrosting Christmas turkey if you are not careful. One Greyhound bitch I know tucked into eight boxes of mince pies and, when her bursting tummy was unable to accommodate the last four pies, she buried them in her bed for later!

DAILY HEALTH CARE

A good diet, a comfortable bed, and parasite control are all basic to the needs of any fit, healthy dog. Regular grooming not only establishes a good relationship between you both, but also reveals any minute changes and unusually sensitive areas on your dog's body.

GROOMING

Greyhound trainers spend a considerable amount of time every day grooming and massaging their racing dogs – and it is a good idea to follow the same, basic procedure. Stand astride your Greyhound's back and use a dandy-brush to take out the old coat. Then use a pair of rubber hound gloves to groom through the coat, massaging the muscles at the same time. Finish by rubbing the coat with a dry towel to bring up the shine.

Regular grooming will keep the coat clean and sleek.

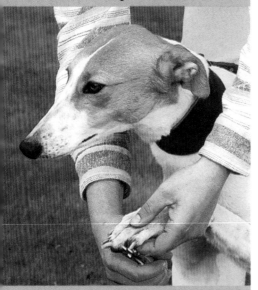

Take care not to probe too deeply when cleaning the ears.

Nails will need to be trimmed on a regular basis.

EARS

If the ears are clean, do not meddle with them, but keep an eye open for excessive wax or black discharge. Wax can be softened and removed with cotton wool (cotton) soaked in olive oil or an ear-cleaner from your vet. In my experience, cotton buds are too intrusive and cause pain. Black discharge may mean the presence of mites, which needs medication from your vet. If there is a smell to the discharge, this may be the first sign of bacteria or yeast infection.

NAILS

These may need clipping if your dog does not walk much on pavements or your dog's feet are 'flat'. If a puppy has not been reared on concrete, the toes do not curl over (like a cat's) and instead the nails project upwards and grow excessively because he does not walk on them. Greyhounds are well-known for screaming alarmingly when their nails are touched by clippers. If your nerves cannot stand it, it is best to ask your vet or grooming parlour to clip them for you.

If you are brave enough to try, use special dog nail-clippers and trim away tiny fragments at a time. Do not forget the dewclaw. A blood vessel goes down the quick of the nail and bleeding and pain can result if too much is cut away. Black nails are the worst because you cannot see the quick in the nail.

TEETH

Greyhounds' teeth are notoriously bad due to muzzling, the sloppy food designed to hydrate them when they are racing, and to the shape of the jaw which allows food to collect over the teeth. Teeth can become so seriously affected that chronic infection can appear in the jawbone and even the heart valves. Good veterinary practices use the ultrasonic method of high-pressure water to clean the teeth and a polisher to leave a smooth, protective surface, which is used in human dentistry.

You can keep your Greyhound's teeth clean by using a soft, angled toothbrush with non-fluoride toothpaste, available from your vet. You can buy a tooth scaler with a sloped chiselled end which you can use to pull off the plaques of tartar – but this can leave a rough surface which encourages tartar formation. Of course, a large, raw marrow bone is ideal for cleaning the back teeth and will give hours of pleasure. This is the only type of bone your dog should have.

If, after the teeth are cleaned, your dog's breath is still foetid, ask the vet to check over your dog's palate and throat, as bad breath can be a sign of some other health problem.

TAIL

Tail-waggers can incur injuries, especially if they have been kept in a confined space like a kennel. A bleeding tail can decorate your wall in a flash! One way of protecting the tip until it heals is to insert it into a hair-curler or the empty barrel of a large syringe, and fix it with sticking plaster.

VACCINATIONS

If your dog comes without a vaccination certificate, this is the first important health matter you must deal with. If your dog was NGRC registered then he will have had his two puppy vaccines and will only need a booster vaccine unless he has been retired more than 18 months. This can be checked with his racing manager or trainer. Otherwise he will need two vaccines. Vaccination protects your dog against distemper, leptospirosis, parvovirus and

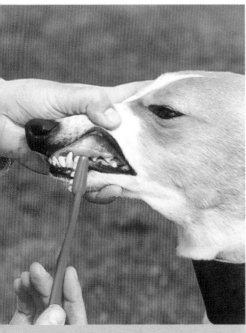

Teeth can be cleaned using a soft, angled toothbrush.

A large marrow bone is ideal or cleaning the back teeth.

infectious hepatitis. In most countries other than the UK, rabies vaccine is a requirement. Booster vaccines need to be given annually throughout the life of your pet. Some brands of vaccine split the components into those which are required annually and those which are only necessary bi-annually so, on alternate years, your booster may be a little cheaper.

PARASITIC CONTROL

FLEAS

When you pick up your dog from the refuge or kennels, assume straightaway that he has fleas and treat him before he infests your carpets. Signs of fleas are little black grains at the base of the fur along his back towards the tail. These are the droppings and they were his blood. Bath your dog immediately! You will be amazed how docile he will be and he will love you for making him feel so much more comfortable. Lift him into six inches of tepid soapy water, with a large towel on the base of the bath to prevent him from slipping. You will need: a mild puppy shampoo, a big jug, a large car sponge and a round, plastic hair massager (to get to the roots of the hair). A shower head, again with tepid water, is a great asset for rinsing out the debris. The fleas will die on contact with the water. Concentrate on his hind parts and his neck where the fleas congregate. Wash his face with plain water and with your hands only; that is the bit he likes least. Rub him vigorously with a towel, comb out the dead fleas with a flea comb, and, when he is dry, spray him with a good flea spray from your vet (if possible, Fipronil) which will protect him for three months from fleas, and is safe for Greyhounds. As a precaution, spray your bathroom and car with room flea-spray, also available from the vet. Avoid organo-phosphous compounds. Do not think you must bath your dog frequently. It is not good for him to lose the natural protective oils in his skin.Bathing once a year is quite enough – unless he makes a habit of rolling in cow-pats!

TICKS
Live ticks bodies can be removed with alcohol e.g. methylated spirits. Wait till the tick dies and remove it carefully, including the head. A retained head can sometimes form an abscess. We scraped off dead ticks like bunches of grapes from the ears and toes of dogs in Spain, using anti-parasitic shampoo. Fipronil spray will protect your dog for one month from tick infestation. Ticks can transmit different diseases depending on which part of the world you live in.

WORMING
Greyhounds can suffer badly from worm infestation in kennels, so it is essential to worm your pet thoroughly on adoption with a combination wormer provided by your vet. Worms are not always visible in the faeces. Regular six-monthly worming is recommended. Loss of condition, poor coat, diarrhoea, weight loss and anal itching can all be signs of worms. Roundworms are the commonest; tapeworms show as small segments round the anus and are often seen together with fleas which act as the intermediate host; hookworms and whipworms can cause anaemia and diarrhoea. My Greyhound Emma, from Ireland, had an unexplained cough on exercise. My clever vet suspected lungworm and this was confirmed on endoscopy. She was successfully cured with a three-week course of worm medication.

A New Lifestyle

Greyhounds would not have the strong urge to chase and kill if these instincts were not deliberately cultivated from birth. Even as pups they are teased and taunted with fluffy toys. At 12 months they are taught to chase after a white rag pulled away from them. Many Greyhounds in Ireland are reared very freely and are left in the countryside to hunt and fend for themselves. One lovely story is told of a prospective owner enquiring after his pups in Ireland. "Well", said the breeder, "I saw them a fortnight ago and they looked alright then!" At the schooling track some Greyhounds are not interested in the artificial lure, either because they are too intelligent or because they are simply bored. These dogs may – illegally – be given a live kill to stimulate them. All this must be borne in mind in order to understand your dog's conditioned behaviour.

Greyhounds come in varying degrees of 'keenness'. Some would not harm any animal whatever; others respond to de-training; while there are those who probably should never be trusted with small animals. Rejected racers, such as non-chasers or 'fighters' – this word usually means that they muck about on the track and want to play with the other dogs instead of concentrating on the chase – often make the easiest pets to adapt to living with small animals.

INTRODUCTIONS

When introducing your cat to your Greyhound, first muzzle the dog. Someone will need to hold the cat in their arms. Make sure the dog's collar is tight and the lead is secure. Two leads and collars can be put on a big strong dog! Have ready a squirt bottle of water that has been kept in the fridge. When the dog lunges towards the cat, squirt his face with water. You will not need to do this more than two or three times before he links his aggressive the dog will not become motivated by the cat running away. Some dogs can be trusted with their own cat but your neighbour's cat may be fair game. Beware, too, of your Greyhound and pet birds. I know of two sad instances of parrots who have been killed within minutes of a Greyhound entering a home straight from racing kennels.

Heaven help you if you are involved in an incident with a small animal and your dog. If you are trying to get your dog to let go of a small animal, pinch his flank or back muscle hard – he will momentarily let go and you have a second to retrieve his prey and redress the situation. Another shock method is to sound one of those aerosol panic alarms with an ear-splitting noise. One variety is called a dog-stop. It may stop your Greyhound in his tracks and may be worth taking out on walks with you in the early days of letting your dog off a lead.

attempts at the cat with the shock of the water on his nose. Praise him when he refrains from attacking the cat. An empty drinks can, filled with pebbles and thrown vigorously on a hard floor, can also shock him out of his 'demonic-like possession'. A courageous cat can teach the dog a lesson by boxing him on the nose! Some cats can be more deadly.

The next stage is to feed the dog and cat together, side by side. Do not trust them alone together, however, until you are sure that

EXERCISE AND WALKS
Your dog will need three or four short walks a day, depending on

how big your own garden is and how much exercise he naturally gets, playing and racing round it. If you do not mind him toiletting in your garden first thing in the morning, last thing at night and after eating, then you can take him for interesting walks, before eating, morning and evening. After vigorous exercise, let him recover his composure first before letting him drink excessively, or eat.

Americans are keen on jogging, bicycling, and even driving with their dogs on leads running beside them. We are not so used to this in the UK – in fact it is rather frowned upon because of the unnatural physical stress to the dog who, in nature, sprints in staccato fashion. They do not have the stamina of a human or a vehicle. Part of the fun of a walk out for the dog is stopping and having a good sniff and reading the 'daily news' of the dog world. Do not let him off the lead for three months at least, or until a strong bond has been formed between you. All sighthounds go slightly deaf when they get their freedom in the country! Remember, too, that a farmer can legally shoot a dog who may threaten or worry his farm stock.

Start teaching your dog to respond to you by first walking two steps away from him when he is still on the lead and calling him, first by his name and then saying "Come". Reward him by praising him and even giving a tidbit when he does respond, however slow that response may have been. Then widen the distance with an extending lead. When you feel more confident, ask a friend to hold the dog a short distance away from you, call him, and release him. If this is successful you can widen the distance even further. Next, train him to wait, unhandled, before you call him. Never punish him when he reaches you, however wayward his journey may have been. His mind is more logical than ours. He connects his last action with your present reaction.

Most Greyhounds are amazingly gentle on the lead and, if you were not looking, you would not even know there was a dog on the end of it. Occasionally you do get one who pulls and, if this is a male or a big female, you need aids to control them. Obedience classes will help, but there are also different kinds of restraints which are helpful.

You may find that a shoulder-harness gives you more control, and it does prevent pulling on the neck. Furthermore, there is a special training harness which combines a collar with straps which go under the armpits. Any tugging, and the straps squeeze the shoulders, so the dog immediately stops pulling. Some people like to use a half-choke or combi-lead which, as the name implies, combines a standard collar with a small double chain which tightens when the dog pulls. The Halti-nose harness is also useful but it must be the narrow version and must be fitted very carefully or the dog can wriggle backwards out of it. It has the added advantage of enabling you to turn the dog's nose and eyes away from the object of interest. Trainers, when controlling their excitable dogs – at the sound of the lure for example – wrap a loop of the attached leather lead under the neck and hold it and the other end either side of the dog's back.

OBEDIENCE CLASSES

I found these invaluable. They teach your Greyhound to socialise and meet other breeds. They teach you how to handle your dog and they are enormous fun. You will be proud of the dog in the

'Downs' and 'Stand-stays' as Greyhounds are so lazy they will not budge anyway! Take a towel or mat that you can carry on your shoulder as you promenade round so that he does not injure the thin skin on his elbows and chest on the 'downs'. Do not force his delicate spine down on the ground but draw him with a tidbit into a down position under a chair and say "Down" when he gets there so he learns to associate that word with his position. My teacher never expected my Greyhounds to sit. Most do not sit naturally as their hind leg muscles are so over-developed and are tense when flexed, and the spine seems too long to be supported by the front legs in a sitting position. Pictures I have seen of Greyhounds sitting show the shoulders bowing outwards awkwardly in order to allow the feet to reach the floor.

The instruction to "Wait" can save your dog's life. Preventing dogs from leaping out of the back of the car as soon as the hatch-back is opened is absolutely essential. With newly-retired dogs I will only allow them to file, one at a time, out of a side door and I leave their leashes on in the car.

Your sighthound will not be a champion in Obedience classes;

you and your dog are more likely to become the comedy act. Hopefully you will have found a teacher who does not take the whole business of Obedience too seriously and considers that lightheartedness and enjoyment are top of the list in priorities. If the floor is too slippery and your dog is terrified of it, or if you become tense and feel on trial yourself, then the classes are no good for you or your dog. He will pick up your tension and become worried and confused. Keep smiling and your dog will relax and be more responsive. Drop out of the class if your dog seems tired. Classes often go on beyond the dog's bedtime.

Agility classes often take place outside on a summer's evening and, in principle, they sound like great fun. You would think that such an athlete as a Greyhound

A shoulder harness will give you greater control.

would be ideal for these classes – but that is not my experience! They were mainly frightened by the tunnel, unsteady on the planks and, as for speed, you would think mine had taken a sleeping tablet. But let me not deter those who have success or who are dedicated to Obedience classes. I am all in favour, as they forge communication between you and your dog, but please do not let competitiveness stand in the way of you both enjoying yourselves and getting to know and trust each other.

GREYHOUNDS AND PLAY

Greyhounds have missed out on a playful puppyhood and have had to mature fast into a stressful adult life. Observing the play of other dogs after retirement can turn them into youngsters again, living out the puppyhood they missed. They find a standard-size ball tricky to hold in their narrow jaws but a larger, squeaky, softer ball is just the thing. Playing tug of war with soft toys, or simply making a collection of them in a basket, is also very popular.

LURE COURSING

We Greyhound owners in the UK are not as familiar with artificial lure coursing as our American neighbours. Other sighthound owners are keener on taking their Whippets, Borzois, Salukis, Afghans, Basenjis and Lurchers to these meetings. I notice, too, that in Germany and Belgium, Greyhound owners affiliate themselves more closely than we do with other sighthound owners.

Many retired Greyhounds have residual injuries from their racing days which render them a risk for this type of pastime. An old minor injury, for instance of one leg, may cause the dog to weigh more heavily on the other leg, causing, perhaps, a major injury to that leg. Have your dog well checked over by a vet who understands Greyhound injuries, or even your local friendly trainer. If you can contact your dog's own trainer you can find out how he ran, whether he interfered with other

These Greyhounds raced in Spain, and are now enjoying life in Germany.

If you become involved with artificial lure coursing, you will be reawakening your Greyhound's chasing instinct.

dogs, what injuries he had and what his racing weight was. Have him checked for heartworm in particular – this is more common in hot climates but is not unknown in the UK. A bitch should not run for 15 weeks following the first show of her season because her ligaments and muscles are weakened by hormonal changes.

The main club in the UK is the British Sighthound Field Association. It is affiliated to the American Sighthound Field Association. They organise meetings at weekends when the weather is clement. They take place on about 14 acres of open field and simulate live-coursing with sweeping bends, zig-zags, circles and straight lines. The course is about 500 to 600 yards and the dogs chase a plastic bag on a running line. Dogs run singly at first at trials, then later in pairs of the same breed together. They are judged on the five attributes of speed, endurance, agility, follow and enthusiasm. There will be a veteran class for dogs over seven years old. In addition, there may be competition classes in Obedience, Agility or breed showing. Racing and showing mix more in the USA than in the UK. A vet will either be present or on call. Other associations exist for running your dog round established tracks at weekends. The precautions are the same in both cases.

Your dog will scream and leap around with excitement when he sees and hears the lure. Do make sure you can hold him, and check his collar and lead for weaknesses. He will need to be muzzled. Remember, you will be cultivating the chase instinct again. Build up his fitness for several weeks beforehand with regular walking and some short sprints. Three or four days ahead, make sure his nails are cut short to prevent him from breaking a toe. On the day, make sure there are no trees or barriers near the bends. The Greyhound is the fastest of the sighthounds and this increased speed brings added dangers,

especially at the bends. Find out where the nearest vet's clinic is and inform the huntsman that your dog is new. Bring plenty of water for drinking and cooling him down. Do not let him race in temperatures above 85 degrees F. Do not feed him before the race or let him drink too much water when he is still stressed after it. Walk him for a few yards after the race to wind down his tense muscle tone. Take some First Aid equipment such as antiseptic cream, bandages and cotton wool padding.

SWIMMING
This activity is particularly good for a race-injured retired dog. As in human physiotherapy, swimming builds up muscles

without the need to weight-bear. Some trainers use warm pools for exercising their racing dogs, and they may allow others to use them too. One very badly injured Greyhound from Spain swims in the summer in the sea in Devon with her owner, and her physique has improved amazingly.

THERAPY DOGS

Greyhounds can make excellent PAT dogs. It is quite a different role for your Greyhound to play , and fulfils a very deep need for sections of the community who are isolated from the rest of us. Long-term prisoners and the mentally ill can often relate better to dogs than to humans. The elderly and the lonely in residential homes may miss their pets, which they could not keep any longer, and eagerly await their canine visitors who brighten their day.

Greyhounds, with their heads at chair height, are very gentle, docile, slow-moving and perfect for being handled by the elderly and frail. The organisers of this scheme only require one quality in a dog – the correct temperament. A PAT dog should be friendly, will come when called by name and will show enjoyment at being stroked or groomed.

Sheeba, a retired racing dog who now works as a therapy 'Pat' dog.

Behavioural Problems

Y our dog needs sufficient exercise, food and secure affection. Absence of any of these can cause fretting, soiling and destructiveness.

TROUBLESHOOTING

One of the saddest facts of home-finding is that dogs often get returned to us and have to be rehomed again. It is a relatively modern phenomenon. Years ago a dog was adopted for life, for better or worse, but, in this disposable modern society tolerance levels are low, expectations are high and the consequence is the recycling of dogs. Family units are unstable, accommodation uncertain, and unemployment and economic instability threaten modern family life. Pets are the first commodity to be jettisoned. It is even sadder that the rejected pet becomes even more difficult to rehome because of added complexes and psychological insecurities arising

out of the rejection. The sensitivity and vulnerability of the dog far outweigh his ability to re-adapt easily to a new environment at each rehoming, and understanding and tolerance are essential to help the dog overcome his anti-social responses to these changes.

ATTACHMENT PROBLEMS

These problems are seen in the panic, destructiveness, soiling, howling and whining of dogs left alone. The problem usually arises because the dog loves you too much. He is not behaving badly out of spite. He panics, hyper-ventilates and is beside himself with anxiety and fear. His toileting become uncontrollable, and he destroys the door and the curtains in an effort to join you. It is usually easy to distinguish the dog who destroys out of boredom and excessive cheekiness from the dog who destroys out of desperation. The desperate dog panics, pants and destroys within minutes of your departure. The bored dog is relaxed and good to start with, but he becomes impatient for your return. If this is the case, try stuffing a hollow rubber toy (known as a kong) with tidbits – it will amuse your dog for hours!

Effective treatment for the anxious dog is the precise opposite of what we would instinctively do. A good long walk is, of course, essential before you leave. Then, for half an hour before you actually depart, completely ignore your dog, invite no eye-contact whatever and just walk out. Leaving unceremoniously prevents the onset of panic and terror – in fact, as you are so horrid, he is quite glad to see you go! If you can, park your car at some distance from the house so that the sound of the engine driving away does not trigger the panic response. Most of the damage is done within the first five minutes of your departure.

When destructiveness and soiling is a problem, place your dog's bed or chair in a confined space like a hallway, or use an indoor crate if you are not out for more than two hours. Otherwise, let the dog have the run of the house, leave lights on and have a tape recording running of routine family noises, or a radio or TV on, to give an air of normality. Leaving unwashed clothes in his bed can help. In the case of soiling, do not feed him till you return. If he does not soil, then feeding him and, obviously, exercising him before you go out can help him to settle. If he drinks excessively, this can be due to his nervousness, so just leave a pint of water to prevent this and the consequent wetting.

When you return, do not make a great fuss of your dog straightaway. If your Greyhound expects a rapturous reunion, this can make him fret all the more. Ignore all misdeeds committed in your absence – he then feels secure and reassured of your unconditional love.

Lisa, a retired racer now living in Holland.

In preparation for separation, prevent your dog from following you everywhere in the house. Have periods at home when there is a closed door between you both for a short while, keeping this exercise as far as possible within the dog's tolerance limits. It may feel harsh to do this but, in the end, the suffering is less for both of you.

TOLERANCE

Make mock departures from the house, like picking up your keys, putting on your coat, then changing your mind and coming back – all, again, within the dog's tolerance level. This helps to desensitise him against the terror caused by your departure and he learns that you will come back.

Kerry was a rescued bitch with a chequered past. She was left alone during the mornings when the family were at work. She soiled in both kinds, even in her owner's bed! Once she emptied everything out of the kitchen cupboards, including an entire bone china dinner service, but strangely did not break one item of it. In desperation, her owners sought the help of an animal behaviourist and the detachment principle was put into action. Within three days she was cured. It was as simple as that! The family continued the strategy for several months until she settled down and was happy and secure.

Some dogs may need the help of medication at first to help with the terror. Beta-blockers are useful drugs in that they block the effects of the fear without sedating the dog, but they do not suit every dog. Anti-anxiety drugs may be used for a limited period but they need to be tailed off very slowly. Some anti-depressant drugs like tricyclics or 5-HT re-uptake inhibitors have been found to be useful in some severe cases.

In the case of a dog who has tolerated separation well but who suddenly starts to fret when parted from you, check his physical well-being in case he is experiencing any discomfort. Deafness, inflamed ears and arthritic pain can cause fretting. An elderly dog may suddenly develop phobic attacks, fear of thunder and fireworks, and restlessness. This may be related to senility. Medication affecting dopamine levels, used in humans for Parkinson's Disease, has been used in America on dogs, with good effect – but it is not yet available for use in the UK.

EXCESSIVE BARKING

Greyhounds are not great barkers. At a chosen time, you can go into a racing kennel where there are 70 dogs and you can hear a pin drop! However, just occasionally, a problem will arise with a pet Greyhound who has found his voice and this can be a problem, particularly when you are out and the neighbours are going spare. To exercise and feed him before you leave are obvious requirements for his comfort. If you have confined him in one room, he may be complaining because you have not given him the run of the house. There is a special French collar called an Aboistop, which emits the scent of citronella when the dog barks. This distracts the dog, who stops barking to investigate the smell. Your vet will be able to supply it. However, it would be unkind to use it on a distressed dog as he will become even more distressed. Never use an electric shock collar. If your dog barks or whines excessively when you are at home, for instance in the early morning, do not reward him by going to him and making a fuss of him. Bang on the door, but do not shout. Then, when he is quiet, go to him and give him a cuddle.

Some dogs who have to be left all day may be happier in commercial kennels. Your local boarding kennels, or even racing kennels, might consider a special rate for day care. Alternatively, a neighbour may be persuaded to come at lunchtime to attend to your dog for a small remuneration.

Adopting a second dog as a companion may help, especially if it is another Greyhound – this is a breed that definitely recognises and relates to its own kind!

Ex-racer Nelson, now living in Switzerland.

AGGRESSION

Most Greyhound owners say that the most common way their dog responds to a visitor at the door is with a yawn! The idea of a Greyhound as a guard dog is more of a joke than a reality. A study conducted by Southampton University, UK, in May 1996 looked at 50 breeds of dog, and rated the Greyhound lowest in aggression. The use of muzzles is misleading – they are used to prevent accidents occuring to racing dogs which are worth a great deal of money. Do become familiar with the Greyhound grin. This may be interpreted as a baring of the teeth when it is, in fact, a delightful expression of pleasure on seeing you. Many dogs, too, snap their teeth together when they are feeling excited, playful or impatient to be taken out for a walk. It often accompanies the play-bow posture. These two gestures are completely non-aggressive.

Uncharacteristic snapping can

Santa a former racer in Spain, now living in the UK.

be the result of some physical discomfort like arthritic pain, earache, or toothache. More serious hidden illnesses, such as kidney or liver disease, cancer of the prostate, or a brain tumour can cause a personality change with unexplained aggression. A bitch, when she has just been spayed, may defend her area because she is in pain. A bitch, too, may act defensively if she is having a false pregnancy. A dog who has recently been neutered may experience hormonal imbalance for about eight weeks while his hormones are changing, and he may exhibit uncharacteristic anti-social behaviour during that time. The failing vision and deafness of old age can cause a dog to snap, having been surprised by someone touching him, especially on the back of the neck, which is the first site of attack by another dog.

All these illustrate that, before a dog is labelled as being snappy, his health should be thoroughly investigated, as he may be trying to tell you that he is not well.

Fear itself can provoke a dog to bite. Skye had been homed straight from a racing kennel and the first morning in her new home she was subjected to the four-year-old child playing with a remote control toy car. Skye was absolutely terrified and took the first opportunity to dash out of the front door. Her new owner chased her for an hour on his bicycle and, having grabbed her, she bit him on both hands. The owner wanted more sympathy from me than for Skye, who was unable to move due to exhausted cramped muscles and bleeding feet. Needless to say, Skye was

Millie, aged 3, in her new home.

rehomed, and she and her new owners were happy for many years. Never was there even a note of aggressive behaviour. The story illustrates how sensitive you must be to dogs who have no previous experience of domestic life. You need to introduce new challenges one at a time.

THE DOMINANT DOG

The dog who will "bite the hand that feeds it" is usually a bossy male who may have been over-indulged by his doting owner. It is rare in Greyhounds, who are generally more submissive as a breed. The dog can become jealous of anyone else taking his owner's attention and may dominate his owner. This happened to Lynne and her male dog, Ibsen. Ibsen was much loved and was always allowed on her bed at night but, after they moved house, Ibsen started to throw his weight around, maybe because he had decided to take over the position of boss in the new premises. He growled at Lynne when she came into the bedroom at night and snapped at her 13-year-old son Matthew when he did not give him some of his TV dinner. Lynne did her homework on male-dominance and decided to relegate Ibsen to the spare room at night. No tidbits were allowed, no demands from Ibsen were heeded and absolute obedience was insisted upon. These Draconian measures were painful both for Lynne and Ibsen, though the growling did cease. It was decided that he should be castrated, which she was advised would solve 70 per cent of the problem. So far this solution has been 100 per cent successful and she has been able to soften her disciplinary measures towards him. She says he is a new dog and, far from being jealous of Matthew, he now chooses to sleep in his room with him.

FIGHTING DOGS

Alas, this can happen between Greyhounds and other breeds living together. There is not always an easy solution. The warning signs are a stiffening of the body; an arched, proud look, particularly of the neck; V-shaped raised hackles along the neck and back; raising of the lip; a high tail or over-excited tail wagging; and eyeballing of the potential victim. Both bitches and dogs can fight, usually with the same sex. The most bitter fighting can be between same-sex siblings, possibly because the usual hierarchy of top dog and underdog is not clear between littermates. Occasionally one hears tragic stories of kennelmates having fought to the death overnight in a racing or a refuge kennel. In the cases I heard of, they shared a bed and we all know how unaware and stupid dogs are about leaving a space for their companions to lie down in. I see it all the time in my car! In a bitch, hormones can be responsible for fighting. The beginning of oestrus and the onset of a phantom pregnancy are dangerous times. I also have experience of a bitch who had always been extremely aggressive to other bitches and who was transformed by spaying. She was found to have polycystic ovaries which destabilised her hormone picture.

Humans, with their own training in democracy, can contribute to friction among multiple dogs by favouring the underdog. Watch your dogs carefully to observe their natural hierarchy and co-operate with it. I do urge you, however, to watch out carefully for any signs of the pack persecuting an ageing or frail

Retired racer Skibs, now living in Greece.

dog. There is a natural pack instinct to destroy the weaker member of the pack. It would be safer to divide the pack when you are not there and place your older dog with a dog you can rely upon to be gentle. Do not nurture possessiveness of beds, toys, etc. Make them multiple, to devalue them, and allow your dogs to swap beds as they wish. Mine swap round every two hours it seems, and take great pleasure in climbing into someone else's warm, smelly bed. In case of a fight, never try to separate the dogs with your bare hands – you run the risk of getting badly bitten. A bucket of water thrown over the pair usually has the desired effect of separating them. When you have to decide to castrate one of two males, be guided by your vet, but it has been suggested that the least dominant male should be castrated to increase the social distance between them, thereby confirming the natural hierarchy.

Do not let these cautionary notes put you off owning a gang of Greyhounds! They love their own kind and a number of problems, like timidity and separation anxiety, naturally resolve when you adopt yet

Jessie, a much-loved family dog, living in the UK.

another Greyhound companion. They are all so easy on the lead and undemanding. Four Greyhounds can be a lot less trouble than one Springer Spaniel! You will have thought, of course, about transportation, the added veterinary costs and holiday arrangements.

TOILET TRAINING

Adopting an adult Greyhound who has lived in kennels all his life brings with it the ticklish problem of house-training. Some, amazingly, adapt straightaway and seem to know instinctively what is required. Others will still regard the floor as a toilet, as they have been accustomed to this in their racing kennel. I believe that all dogs can be trained in the end, with patience, understanding and the right home. If a dog is being particularly difficult in this respect, have him checked by a vet for any other reasons which may cause incontinence, such as cystitis or worms. Taking a specimen of his urine to the vet will help the diagnosis. Worm him with tablets bought from your vet, not from a pet shop. It is not uncommon for homefinders to have to remove a dog from one home for being 'dirty' and then to find that the dog is immediately 'clean' in the new home, with no effort apparently spent at all on the problem. It is hard to know for certain why this is.

A dog who is defaulting needs vigilance and time devoted to him, in order positively to train him; that means careful observation of the signs when he is about to

excrete, like sniffing, or circling. Quickly take him outside to perform and then praise him and play with him. Wherever there has been a previous accident, there is the temptation to repeat it in the same place. Make up a stock solution of cold water with biological detergent and sponge it on the area. Ammonia-based cleaners smell like urine to a dog. Disinfectants are not necessary. They can stain your carpet permanently. Urine is, or should be, sterile. Carpet stain removers can deal with fatty deposits. There are special deodorisers which you can buy from your vet for the purpose. Feeding the dog in that place afterwards will also help to prevent a repetition there.

Dogs can be taught to defecate in a place chosen by you and trained to perform to the repetition of a command such as "Get busy". Of course, the optimum time after a meal should be chosen. You will be able to anticipate the workings of your dog's digestive system if you feed him at a regular time each day and observe him carefully. If he defecates in the night, feed him earlier in the day so he empties

Former Spanish racer Abbey, at home in Dartmoor, UK.

earlier. Feeding a low-residue, concentrated diet, which reduces bulk and the urge to evacuate frequently, can help. In severe cases you may need to confine or crate your dog. He will hardly ever soil his sleeping area. Take him out every hour, stay with him until he performs and then praise and play with him when he does.

Retired British racer Stevie, now living in the USA.

Never punish your dog after the event. They have very short memories and will not know why you are angry. Neither rub the dog's nose in it, nor hit your dog. These punishments will only promote more confusion and fear and, consequently, more accidents.

You will find it useful in time to encourage your dog to 'get busy' on different surfaces like grass, concrete or sand, for the times when you are away from home or for when the dog goes into boarding kennels and the runs are concrete.

Always clear up after you dog. This is essential if dogs are to be socially acceptable in the community.

COPROPHAGIA

Some dogs eat their own faeces or that of another species, either as a way of supplementing energy intake or as an inborn habit, possibly due to hunger in the past. It seems to do no harm but it is unpleasant and the breath smells disgusting. No amount of disciplining seems to stop them. Try distracting your dog instead. Removing or avoiding the opportunity is one obvious remedy. Feed your dog several smaller meals a day to avoid hunger and feed a high-fibre diet which makes his own faeces less attractive. Always leaving a supply of complete food available would help, provided you do not own another dog such as a Labrador, who would become gross on it! If the dog eats his own droppings, then your vet can suggest a mineral supplement like iron which makes the stool taste unpleasant.

THE TIMID DOG

We have all seen the trembling Greyhound who flattens himself against the back wall of the kennel and is almost impossible to cajole out into the open. It is very heartening to find an owner, who is sufficiently moved by this behaviour, and dedicated, adopting such a dog, as they are often mistrustful and slow to respond to your loving approaches for some time. Why are some like this, while others are full of confidence and joie de vivre?

Some carry a timid gene in the breeding. Others may not have been sufficiently socialised as pups. In Ireland, where thousands are bred before transportation to the UK, many are reared on farms and allowed to run wild over the fields for many months. They rarely come into contact with humans and have missed out on being handled in those vital young, formative days. They do, however, become good chasers and racers, but

Retired racer Roger, now living in Holland.

domestication is far from their experience. A trainer I know in the UK, who has bred hundreds of pups, has not encountered timidity in any of hers. They are handled from the first day, and owners and visitors are encouraged to walk round the kennels petting and talking to all her dogs.

The timid dog is risky to handle from the first day because of his fear and the urge to run away, so great care must be taken and not one mistake made, such as momentarily opening your front door unguardedly. The dog must wear an identity tag from the moment he is taken from the security of his kennel and must wear his collar, fitted cosily at the narrowest part of the neck, at all times in the house. Leave his lead attached in the car to grab it when disembarking him. A timid dog will gain in confidence more quickly in the company of other confident dogs. He will copy them and will see how they approach you and how harmless you are.

The timid Greyhound will learn that he does not have to crawl on his belly before you. Do not fuss him too much, or feed his anxieties with sympathy. Let him come to you when he is ready. The best approach is to adopt a cheerful, no-nonsense manner and to be fairly firm so that your dog feels secure. Avoid eye contact at first, and discourage any attempts to hide away. Keep to a regular routine, so that your Greyhound knows what to expect.

For a timid dog living on his own, progress may be slower. If you use an indoor crate in the main living room, the dog can view comings and goings from the security of his own 'den', and it will also curb his desire to retreat and hide behind the sofa.

Greyhounds have a naturally low thyroxine level, and research has shown that nervous dogs have an even lower level. In some cases, thyroxine supplements have been prescribed with good results. Other remedies that have proved successful include Brewers yeast and Bach flower remedies.

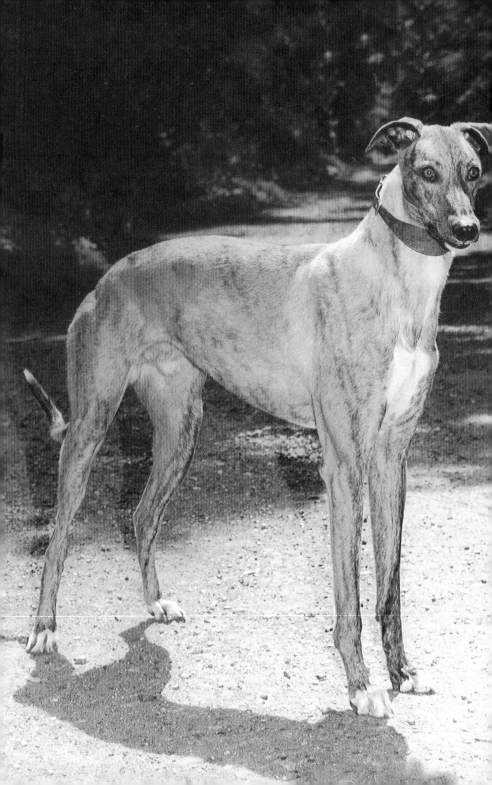

Health Care

On first adopting your Greyhound, you should take him along to your chosen vet to introduce yourself and your dog and to have him registered and checked. All practices in the UK are obliged to offer a 24-hour emergency service. Some Greyhounds may be afraid of a male vet due to previous experience with men in the racing industry. There are many female vets in practice – and all vets are used to being feared by their patients! Veterinary care will cost you money. Vets are highly-trained people and should not be expected to work for nothing.

In the UK we are used to free medical treatment, which gives us a false idea of how much good medical treatment actually costs. I have mentioned before the advantages of pet insurance. If you cannot afford veterinary treatment or insurance then you should really not consider adopting any animal. Many vets will accept payment in instalments. In the UK, the Blue Cross, the RSPCA and

the PDSA have clinics for those who cannot pay. They may ask for proof of entitlement to State benefits and they may be based at some distance from you and you will need transport. They are only open for limited periods, and may not be able to help in an emergency. Other countries have their own charity-based systems of support.

Some veterinary practices specialise in Greyhounds, as they are attached to a racing track. The racing manager or a trainer will be able to recommend a good Greyhound vet. He can be very helpful in diagnosing orthopaedic and metabolic problems associated with your dog's racing years.

A-Z OF AILMENTS

ANAESTHETICS

If your dog ever needs a general anaesthetic, make sure, tactfully, that your vet understands the special hazards of anaesthetising a dog with very little body fat, such as a Greyhound. You could show him this book! Barbiturate, commonly used for inducing anaesthesia, can kill a Greyhound, as his lean body is unable to get rid of the drug, which keeps circulating round the system delaying his recovery. The dog may suffer a heart attack or never recover from the anaesthetic. Many vets nowadays use propofol or isoflurane for all their patients. These are safe for Greyhounds, but they are expensive. If your dog needs an anaesthetic for neutering or anything else, it is wise to have his teeth cleaned at the same time, which is good for your dog's health and your pocket in the long run.

ANAL GLANDS

These are scent glands located either side of the anal opening and should empty naturally as a stool is passed. They can become impacted with age or with soft diets and become hard and uncomfortable. They may need to be expressed manually by your vet, who could teach you how to do it. If the condition becomes chronic, an injection into the gland, or an excision under anaesthetic, may be necessary.

ARTHRITIS

Dogs who have participated in competitive racing will commonly suffer from early arthritis. While racing, the dog sustains trauma to the smaller limb joints, e.g. wrist, hock and toes, but advancing age finds the problems located in the larger joints, e.g. shoulder, elbow, hip and stifle. Clinical signs are stiffness and a reluctance by the dog to get up out of his basket. The joints may be swollen, tender and warm to the touch. The problem may be exacerbated by cold, wet weather.

Your vet will be able to help with pain-killers and anti-inflammatory medicines which will help your dog's appreciation of life tremendously. Tablets of Arnica, one four times a day on an empty stomach, is a useful remedy, and Arnica cream or lotion on the joint can relieve pain and inflammation. Evening primrose oil may be of some benefit.

Check your Greyhound on a routine basis, and then you will spot any signs of trouble at an early stage.

BALANITIS

This is an infection of the penis and sheath. The discharge becomes thick and yellow-green coloured and the dog may even have tonsillitis from licking himself. It may cause a bladder or kidney infection with signs of frequency of urination or blood-stained urine. Cystitis is also commonly seen in the bitch and can be very acute and uncomfortable. If you suspect any of these problems, then veterinary treatment with antibiotics is required. A specimen of urine in a perfectly clean bottle or disposable plastic cup will help your vet with the diagnosis. Some degree of kidney failure can be a problem of middle and old age. The dog may drink and urinate excessively. Your vet will do tests. A low-protein, good-quality diet of cooked white meat or fish may be all that is needed for maintenance. If a male dog shows signs of difficulty with urinating, seek help immediately. A stone may be blocking the urethra, which is both painful and dangerous as it can lead to a ruptured bladder.

BALD THIGH SYNDROME

A lot has been written about this condition in Greyhounds. Many causes have been suggested: the stress of racing causing hormone imbalance; old sarcoptic mange; kennel rubbing; or urine scalding. Many dogs will revert to normal hair production after a few months of happy retirement as a pet. Some owners swear by

A balanced diet and regular exercise will keep your dog in good health.

evening primrose oil tablets (Efavet) for at least a month. Others give small quantities of fish oil by mouth (like tins of sardines). Trainers traditionally rub in Benzyl Benzoate. A specialist Greyhound vet may be interested in looking at the dog's thyroxine levels and giving thyroxine tablets. The fact is that once a Greyhound has retired, and lives in a home, there are many changes to which his metabolism and coat must adjust – indoor warmth, different food, less physical stress, more individual attention and love. His coat will reflect this, just as in humans our skin reflects our inner well-being, or lack of it. His coat may shed at first, and regrow, sometimes with a richer colouring and different texture, so be patient, watch and wait!

BONE CANCER

Bone cancer seems to be increasingly common among Greyhounds, maybe because of knocks they get while racing or maybe because of their large bone mass. The first signs are pain and lameness, with or without a swelling. The diagnosis is confirmed on X-ray. Veterinary treatment can really only be palliative, but many devoted owners will turn to alternative medicine and will spare no expense in search of help for their pet. However, the condition is very painful, and the owner should be aware that the cancer may spread elsewhere. Swellings at any site or unexplained weight loss should always be investigated.

Brain tumours are not unknown in Greyhounds and, I think, should be suspected if there is a sudden deterioration in behaviour, or, the dog becomes uncharacteristically aggressive or destructive. This type of tumour is very difficult to diagnose unless the dog has a special scan at a veterinary hospital.

CATARACTS

This shows as a greying of the normal black pupil of the eye, with subsequent reduction in vision. The compensating enhancement of the dog's other senses of smell, hearing, temperature detection and familiarity with his home environment often means that this failure of sight is undetected by the owner, but if the dog is moved to a strange environment, such as a kennel or another home, he may show signs of distress. This may baffle the owner because the blindness was unappreciated.

DIARRHOEA

Several different organisms can cause diarrhoea. Scavenging is a common cause. If the faeces becomes bloody, or if vomiting persists, contact your vet immediately. Some stomach upsets resolve naturally. Keep your pet hydrated with a mixture of water and glucose (or sugar) and a few grains of salt. I found once that the water used to poach smoked haddock appealed to my sick dog when I could not get her to take anything else. You can use a large syringe or a vessel with a narrow neck to drip the fluid into the side of the mouth.

When your pet feels better, he may be able to eat cooked rice and fish. Parvovirus and haemorrhagic gastro-enteritis are more serious gastric diseases which can be fatal. Giardia is an organism which can be detected in a sample of stool and needs specific treatment. Cleaning feeding bowls thoroughly, especially if you have multiple dogs, is extremely important.

EPILEPSY

This can develop in the dog due to a tumour, accident, metabolic disease or it may be unexplained. It is very distressing and frightening for the owner. The dog will not remember anything except a 'black-out'. If you are there when it happens, do not touch the dog. Dim the lights, open a window and try to prevent him damaging himself as he convulses. He may be unsteady and confused after the fit but will be back to normal within an hour. He may be ravenously hungry after a fit. Do not fuss over him too much or he may think that something is wrong, become confused and go into another fit. Anti-convulsant drugs or sedation may be considered by your vet if the fits become frequent.

EXERTIONAL RHABDOMYOLYSIS

This condition is also called azoturia or 'tying up', and it is well-known to all who race Greyhounds. It is a serious form of muscle exhaustion, with varying levels of acuteness. It happens, particularly in warm weather, to unfit dogs, excitable dogs or to those who race too frequently. Panting causes hyperventilation and acidosis in the blood due to over-oxygenation, and the intense exercise causes changes in the muscle membranes so that they leak enzymes. If there is red urine post-racing, then this shows that there has been some muscle damage. The dog cramps up within 24 hours of the race and is in extreme pain, especially down the back and the neck. The danger is that the heart muscle also becomes damaged and the kidneys block up with the precipitate in the urine. Death can result.

Intravenous fluids (not lactated), sodium bicarbonate, antibiotics, cold compresses to the muscles, anti-inflammatories, anabolic steroids and vitamins can all help redress the situation. On no account allow hydrocortisone to be given, which is a catabolic steroid. Do not race your dog again if this condition has ever occurred.

GASTRIC TORSION (BLOAT)

This is a serious, life-threatening condition most commonly seen in deep-chested dogs like Greyhounds. The stomach first dilates with gas and fluid, then becomes twisted. Signs are panting, vain attempts at vomiting, restlessness and visible abdominal distension with drum-like tightness just below the ribs. The dog should be taken immediately to the vet for emergency surgery. Nobody is absolutely certain what causes it. A large intake of dry food or water, especially after exercise, has been suggested as one possible cause. Divide meals into two or three a day and do not allow your dog to eat or drink too much when he is still stressed from exercise.

HEART AND LUNG DISEASE

When a Greyhound races, he runs his heart out. It is alarming to listen to the sound effects at close range beside the track as the dogs race past at nearly 40 mph and even more alarming to watch them come off the track, gasping for air and with their faces covered in sand! There is no doubt that they enjoy the race, but they are not permitted to race more than once in five days in the UK because of the stress to their systems. Sometimes Greyhounds

develop heart defects which catch up with them in later life. Cough and lethargy, with fluid accumulation round the abdomen, can be signs of a heart problem. Your vet will be able to prescribe medicine which can help the condition a great deal.

Incidences of stroke are an unfortunate consequence of a clot or bleeding in the brain or the spinal cord. Paralysis of the limbs results and the dog may be otherwise completely well, eating and wagging his tail, but simply unable to get up, defecate or urinate. Some recovery may occur over a week or so. Be guided by your vet as to how long it is reasonable to wait. I know someone whose Greyhound took two to three months to learn to walk again. She has no regrets at waiting for the recovery.

I have known a dog who suffered lung damage due to the toxic fumes from the excessive use of disinfectant in kennels. If the disinfectant gets trapped under the bench and is not swept away, then the dog can suffer an overdose of it. The dog was treated over a long period by a vet and recovered well enough to enjoy a somewhat shortened life.

HEATSTROKE

Greyhounds are sensitive to both cold and heat, not having much natural insulation. A dog whose temperature rises to 42-43 degrees Centigrade, even for a few minutes (the normal is 38.5 C), can collapse and die. Being left in a hot room or vehicle can cause death within ten minutes. Signs are distress, frantic panting and collapse. It is an acute emergency. Cool the dog as fast as possible with copious amounts of ice-cold water to the head and the back, massaging the water into the coat so there is not a blanket of water over him. Wet towels, a hose, a paddling pool, or a river will all do in an emergency. In hot weather your dog needs water every 30-60 minutes to replace the fluid lost by panting. Always carry a two-litre can of water in your car when you transport your dog – you never know when you are going to be caught in a traffic jam in sunny weather.

LARYNGEAL PARALYSIS

This is a degenerative disease of the nerves serving the vocal cords which become paralysed and cause airway obstruction with noisy breathing. It is especially noticeable in hot weather and after exercise when the dog needs to pant quickly. It is known in race-horses and long-necked dogs. Surgery, usually done by a specialised surgeon, is needed to tie back one of the cords to allow easier air entry. Our Emma had it done and it gave her a new lease of life of several more years.

MANGE

By far the commonest skin problem is sarcoptic mange which is very difficult to eradicate entirely in a racing kennel, due to the participation of dogs from all over the country who use the track. The disease is very infectious between dogs and is due to a mite which burrows under the skin, causing baldness, redness and intense itching. Treatment is with an anti-parasitical shampoo or dip from your vet, repeated at intervals, and is effective. Demodectic mange is less common in the adult dog. It commonly affects the face and forelegs and causes balding but not itching. It can be a problem in older dogs if the immune system is suppressed by illness or by stress. Treatment can be difficult in such a case.

PROBLEMS OF THE REPRODUCTIVE ORGANS

An undescended testicle (cryptorchidism) is a risk to the dog because it is subject to disease, especially cancer. Your vet would recommend castration. Infection, enlargement or cancer of the prostate cause abdominal pain and depression, and there may be some bowel, or urinary straining due to the internal pressure on these organs. Your vet would be able to detect it on rectal examination. Treatment depends on the cause of the disease.

Mammary tumours are not all malignant and are usually removed surgically. They occur much less often in a spayed bitch. Spaying, which is the removal of the uterus and ovaries, also has the advantage of preventing the serious disease, pyometra, which is an infection of the uterus following a heat (oestrus). Fever, loss of appetite and increased thirst are signs to beware of. The uterus fills with pus which enters the blood – stream. Treatment is with antibiotics and ovariohysterectomy, but the bitch will be very seriously ill. Spaying could have prevented this.

Spaying/castration also protects

your dog from the desire to escape to find a mate, often ending tragically in road traffic accidents. Breeding from your dog should be out of the question when there are thousands of unfortunate Greyhounds already in refuge kennels and needing homes.

It is important to spay a bitch at the correct time in her cycle. The best time is three months after her first day of bleeding. If she has been spayed earlier than that, her hormones may be halted at the lactation phase, and she may be, temperamentally, in a permanent state of phantom pregnancy, with nesting instincts, anxiety and even aggression. If this is the case, a drug can be given to lower the prolactin level and correct the problem.

Greyhound bitches start their seasons at about 9-18 months old. The cycle may be 6-, 9- or 12-monthly, or even longer. The stress of racing may postpone their season until a period of rest, which is why so many recently-retired bitches immediately come into season. Seasons may have been suppressed which can disrupt the normal cycle. The cycle comprises the three-week period of oestrus, followed by a three-week period of normality followed by the nine-week lactation period. The mammary glands may or may not swell. If you have to cope with a bitch in season, remember she is at her greatest risk for a week any time from the fifth day of bleeding to the end at 21 days. If an unwanted mating occurs, your vet can give a series of injections to prevent the egg implanting itself, but only up to three days after the misalliance. An injection can be given to your bitch to prevent her season but prolonged use, year after year, is not advisable.

The Last Years

A Greyhound can live to 15 years or more. I notice that imported dogs from Spain have shorter lives. Your dog will need more veterinary care as he grows older and you owe it to him not to deny him anything that will make life more tolerable for him in his last years. Above all, do not abandon him! You may think this is impossible, but I recently removed a dog, 12 years old, from a wet, cold kennel in a refuge. He had been returned there after spending ten years with one family. At 12, a dog requires only comfortable, familiar surroundings, regular food and a little exercise. He will mainly sleep all day. Uprooting him has caused almost intractable anxiety and phobias in this once contented, undemanding dog.

More commonly, owners dread the day when they must part with their beloved companion. It is hard to face the fact that a dog's life is shorter than ours, and more than once in a lifetime we may suffer the pain of losing a companion who has found his way so deeply into our hearts and lives.

DECIDING ON EUTHANASIA

The time may come when you have to decide whether euthanasia is right for your dog. The decision is usually made with the sensitive help of your vet, who will be experienced in handling such a situation and can sometimes see more clearly than you that an animal's life should not be prolonged. Although euthanasia should not be based on convenience, your own situation does need to be taken into account: whether you are out working; whether there are financial constraints; whether there are children and the animal is incontinent; or whether or not you are becoming seriously distressed yourself by nursing your sick pet. Ask yourself a few questions. Has he lost his

appetite? Is it a long time since he wagged his tail? Is he in pain? Does he no longer sleep soundly? Is he incontinent? Does he have breathing difficulties? If the answer is yes to any of those questions then, maybe, euthanasia should be considered.

Sit down with the family or an experienced friend and think ahead how you will deal with the situation. All too often the distress is so great that you get carried along by tears and the persuasion of others and then you may reproach yourself for not having carried it out differently. There is quite enough pain afterwards without added guilt.

I believe you should involve the children in the decision-making and give them the opportunity of saying goodbye to their pet. This will be painful for you to watch, but it will help their mourning process in the long run. It is hard to know what sort of expression to use to explain euthanasia to a child. However, 'put to sleep' or 'special injection' or 'gone to heaven' are all terms that can be understood.

Talk to your vet about where and when you want it to take place. I personally favour the vet coming to the house to give the injection. The dog simply drifts off 'to sleep' in his own basket. Not all practices offer this service and it does cost more.

Alternatively, the vet may come to your car, which is still friendly and familiar territory for your dog. This also saves you the agony of entering a surgery full of people. It is very upsetting for them too. If neither of these are possible, then ask if you can take your pet out of surgery hours.

Think ahead about whether you want to be present during the injection. It is obviously better for your pet if you are, but do try and smile at him and talk reassuringly to allay his fears. Think of the joys that pet ownership has brought to you and embrace him firmly with gratitude. When a dog is sick, his veins collapse and it is sometimes difficult to give the injection. That is why it is easier sometimes to have the dog standing so the veins are more prominent. In the surgery, standing is more natural for your dog anyway, rather than forcing him into a lying position. He will sink slowly into your arms.

GRIEVING

Think what you will do with the body. If you have a big garden,
you may wish to bury him there. Your Environmental Health office will give advice. You may ask for individual cremation and you can request the ashes which will be given to you in a sealed casket. Otherwise the body of your pet will be collected from the vet's surgery and cremated in a purpose-built incinerator.

If you have children it is a good idea to have a burial ceremony in the garden and to plant a monument of some kind with flowers beside it. Be as positive as possible, saying he has gone back to nature, is not in pain anymore and is now at peace. Creating an album of his life can be therapeutic and helpful for children.

The pain of losing a pet should not be underestimated. People who laugh and say "but it was only a dog" should be pitied. At your worst moments you may feel you are in a black void from which you will never recover. Keep your feet firmly on the ground and let the tears flow freely. Be comforted. Hundreds of us have been there before. You will get over it.

For some who have experienced a previous painful human loss, the wound can be reopened. If, after a few weeks, you find you are simply not coping, do consider consulting your doctor who may surprise you with his understanding of your feelings. Alternatively, there are pet bereavement counsellors trained in helping people in your situation. Your veterinary surgery or one of the large animal charities will be able to put you in touch with someone.

GETTING ANOTHER DOG

Some people feel that they cannot live without a dog and will adopt a replacement almost immediately. For those who would choose a Greyhound, this is always welcomed as there are so many thousands longing for adoption. Others may need time to mourn and recover before being able to accept another.

A retired couple I know lost Gyp from cancer. Peter phoned me within a few days to offer a home to another dog. On my arrival with Souki, Joan, his wife, was obviously too distressed about Gyp to be able to respond to Souki. Peter persevered and eventually, after six months, Joan opened up to Souki, accepted her and was indeed grateful to Peter for adopting her and for their patience in waiting for her to be able to respond. The loss of Gyp was no easier for Peter than for Joan but Peter had had five dogs before, whereas Gyp was Joan's first dog in adult life and the bond went very deep indeed. The adoption of a new dog does not detract from the love and memory of your deceased pet. You will find you can love your new pet equally alongside his memory.

There is safety in numbers. Some people may adopt a younger dog as the existing one is approaching old age. This will often give your old dog a new lease of life, and the presence of the younger dog helps considerably to overcome the grief when the old dog dies. Remember all the joy and benefits of owning a dog. A dog relaxes you and improves your health by encouraging exercise and lowering your blood pressure; a dog brings humour, fulfils your caring instincts and teaches you about health matters; he makes it easier for you to make human friends who share the same interest and is especially meaningful for those who are lonely or who have lost human loved ones.

May you continue to enjoy the sweetness, beauty and grace of this regal breed of dog, the Greyhound.

FURTHER READING

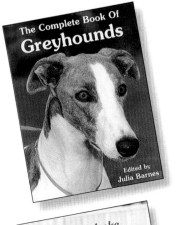

The Complete Book of GREYHOUNDS

A definitive Book of the Breed, giving detailed information on Greyhound Care, as well as highlighting the life of the racing Greyhound. Lavishly illustrated with colour and black and white photographs.

Price £17.50

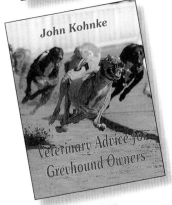

Veterinary Advice For GREYHOUND OWNERS

The answers to a host of queries relating to your greyhound's health, written by John Kohnke, the veterinary columnist in the Greyhound Star newspaper.

Price £14.99

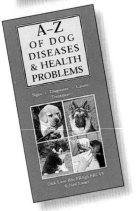

A-Z of DOG DISEASES and HEALTH PROBLEMS

The definitive work on health care. Written by Guide Dogs for the Blind veterinary consultant Dick Lane and breeding manager Neil Ewart.

Price £14.99

Ringpress Books, PO Box 8, Lydney, Gloucestershire, GL15 6YD, United Kingdom.